"A WORLD WITH A BETTER HUMANITY IS POSSIBLE."

— José Mujica

T0082105

Published in English in Canada and the USA in 2024 by Groundwood Books.
First published in Spanish as *José Mujica: Soy del Sur, vengo del Sur. Esquina del Atlántico y el Plata* copyright © 2019 by AKIARA books, SLU, Barcelona, Spain
Analysis text copyright © 2019 by Dolors Camats
Illustrations copyright © 2019 by Raúl Nieto Guridi
Translation copyright © 2024 by Sofía Jarrín
Translation rights arranged through the VeroK Agency, Barcelona, Spain

José Mujica's 2013 United Nations Assembly address has been adapted for a middle-grade audience.
Cultural sensitivity read by Sofía Jarrín

All rights reserved. No part of this publication may be reproduced, stored in a retrieval system or transmitted, in any form or by any means, without the prior written consent of the publisher or a license from The Canadian Copyright Licensing Agency (Access Copyright). For an Access Copyright license, visit www.accesscopyright.ca or call toll free to 1-800-893-5777.

Groundwood Books / House of Anansi Press
groundwoodbooks.com

We gratefully acknowledge for their financial support of our publishing program the Canada Council for the Arts, the Ontario Arts Council and the Government of Canada.

Canada Council for the Arts   Conseil des Arts du Canada

ONTARIO ARTS COUNCIL
CONSEIL DES ARTS DE L'ONTARIO
an Ontario government agency
un organisme du gouvernement de l'Ontario

With the participation of the Government of Canada
Avec la participation du gouvernement du Canada | Canadä

Library and Archives Canada Cataloguing in Publication

Title: José speaks out / speech by José Mujica ; commentary by Dolors Camats ; translation by Sofía Jarrín ; illustrations by Guridi.
Other titles: Soy del sur, vengo del sur. English
Names: Mujica Cordano, José Alberto, 1934- author. | Camats, Dolors, writer of added commentary. | Jarrín, Sofía, translator. | Nieto Guridi, Raúl, illustrator.
Series: Speak out series (Groundwood Books (Firm)) ; 4.
Description: Series statement: Speak out ; 4 | Translation of: Soy del sur, vengo del sur. Esquina del Atlántico y el Plata. | Includes bibliographical references. | Text in English. Translated from the Spanish.
Identifiers: Canadiana (print) 2023049109X | Canadiana (ebook) 20230491103 | ISBN 9781773067254 (hardcover) | ISBN 9781773067261 (EPUB) | ISBN 9781773067278 (Kindle)
Subjects: LCSH: Mujica Cordano, José Alberto, 1934—Juvenile literature. | LCSH: Environmental justice—Juvenile literature. | LCSH: Environmental protection—Juvenile literature. | LCSH: Environmentalism—Juvenile literature. | LCSH: Environmentalists—Juvenile literature. | LCGFT: Speeches.
Classification: LCC GE220 .M8513 2024 | DDC j363.7—dc23

The poem "El sur también existe" on page 46 was written by Mario Benedetti in 1985.

The illustrations were created using ink and brush with digital retouching.
Design by Inês Castel-Branco and Danielle Arbour
Printed and bound in South Korea

MIX
Paper | Supporting responsible forestry
FSC
www.fsc.org   FSC® C140526

JOSÉ
SPEAKS OUT

Speech by José Mujica | Commentary by Dolors Camats
Translation by Sofía Jarrín | Illustrations by Guridi

GROUNDWOOD BOOKS   HOUSE OF ANANSI PRESS   TORONTO / BERKELEY

Contents

SPEECH

KEYS TO THE SPEECH

José Mujica's Speech Before the United Nations Assembly

New York, September 24, 2013

Dear friends,

I am from the South, I come from the South. My country is on the corner of the Atlantic and La Plata River. It's a gentle, temperate, large expansion of land, ideal for cattle breeding. Its history — of shipping ports, hides, jerky, wool and beef — also had violent decades of spears and horses, until finally, at the beginning of the twentieth century, it became a country at the cutting edge of social, state and educational issues. I would even dare say that social democracy was invented in Uruguay.

For close to fifty years, the world looked at us with admiration, comparing us to Switzerland when in fact, economically speaking, we were an informal colony of the British Empire. Then, when the British Empire fell, we experienced the bitter honey of unfavorable terms of trade. We were left longing for the past, remembering our World Cup win at Maracanã Stadium. Today, we have reemerged in this globalized world, having learned from our heartbreak.

My personal story is the story of a young man — because I was once a young man — who wanted like many others to change the world, and had a dream of a free, classless society. The mistakes I made are partly a consequence of the times I had to live in. I recognize them as my own mistakes, indeed, but there are times when I cry out with nostalgia: "If only we had the strength of the past, when we were always reading, studying and imagining a utopian society together!"

However, I refuse to look back because today's reality was born from yesterday's fertile ashes. On the contrary, I'm not interested in collecting past debts nor rehashing the past. I feel great anguish because of a future that I will not get to see but to which I am committed. Yes, a world with a better humanity is possible, but perhaps today our main task is to save lives.

I am from the South, and from the South I have come before this assembly to share my thoughts. I see and feel responsible for the poverty of millions who live in urban areas, in the mountains, in the rainforests, in the pampas and in the underground mines of Latin America, a common homeland in the making. I see and feel responsible for oppressed Indigenous peoples, for the Malvinas Islands crushed by colonialism and for the useless blockades against Cuba. I also feel a duty to warn against electronic

surveillance, which does nothing but create mistrust, a mistrust that is needlessly poisoning us. I feel a duty toward an enormous social debt and the need to defend the Amazon, the seas and our great rivers of the Americas.

I also feel a duty to fight for a homeland for all and for a peaceful Colombia. And I feel a duty to fight for tolerance, a necessary tolerance for those who are different and with whom we have differences and disagreements. Tolerance is not necessary when we agree on things. Tolerance is the foundation of a peaceful coexistence and the understanding that in this world, we are all different.

When it comes to fighting against the illegal economy, drug trafficking, swindling, fraud and corruption — all modern plagues that affect us when we illogically believe that we are happier when we are richer, by any means necessary — we have sacrificed old spiritual gods to adorn our temples with the God of the Market. He organizes our economy, politics, habits, life. He also gives us the illusion that happiness can be bought in installments and with credit cards. It would seem we were born to consume and consume and, when we can no longer consume, we are overcome with frustration, poverty and even self-isolation.

The truth is that today, if everyone consumed like the average person in the United States, we would need three planets to survive. In other words, we have been tricked by the promises of our civilization. The way we are going, we won't be able to fulfill our endless need for wasteful products. Is that how we value life? In fact, we are permanently guided by mass consumption and endless accumulation.

We have been promised a life of waste, which essentially leads to a countdown against nature and the future of human life on this planet. It's a civilization against simplicity, against sobriety, against nature's cycles, and even worse, it's a civilization against freedom and the hope that we will have time to experience transcendental human relationships: love, friendship, adventure, solidarity and family. It's a civilization against free time — that is, time we don't have to pay for and don't have to buy — time for contemplation and to experience the natural world. We are razing the rainforests, the real rainforests, to build concrete jungles where everyone is anonymous. We try to overcome sedentary lifestyles with treadmills, insomnia with sleeping pills and loneliness with electronics. We should be asking ourselves instead: are we truly happy cut off from what it means to be human? We avoid our human purpose — which is to defend life for life's sake — and replace it with just becoming consumers with the need to accumulate things.

Politics, the eternal mother of all human affairs, has been enslaved to the economy and the financial market. Instead of striving to change things, politicians have delegated their power and fight, bewildered, for who controls the government. And we march on, uncontrollably, as if in a human comedy, buying and selling everything and somehow finding new ways to negotiate even those things that are nonnegotiable. Marketing is used for everything: for cemeteries, funeral services, maternity wards, for fathers and mothers, for grandparents and uncles, to hire people,

cars and vacations ... everything, everything is for profit.

And even worse, marketing campaigns are now deliberately targeting children, manipulating them into influencing their parents, and manipulating the children themselves into becoming consumers of the future. There is plenty of evidence about how these rather harmful technologies lead to frustration ... and sometimes even kill.

The average person wanders in our big cities between financial buildings and the boring routine of their workplace, sometimes cooled by air-conditioning. They dream of vacations, freedom and paying off their debts. Until one day their heart stops, and they have to say goodbye to this world. There will always be another soldier to face the jaws of the market, to make sure consumerism continues.

Today's political crisis is a globalized economy that doesn't understand that people will always have strong feelings of nationalism for the places they come from.

But today is the time to start fighting back, to make way for a world without borders. The globalized economy has no other interest than making a few people rich, and each nation is only interested in its own stability and continuity, while the goal of all nations should be instead to focus on everyone on the planet as a whole. To make it worse, instead of a global market that produces abundantly for everyone, we have a financial market imprisoned by the big banks, owned by the richest nations.

More clearly, let's say it more clearly: we believe that the world is crying out for global rules that respect scientific achievements, but science does not govern the world. We need, instead, to come up with policies and answers to these questions together: how many hours should we all work collectively on Earth, as a whole? How could our currencies come together? How could we finance global efforts to protect water sources and fight against droughts? How do we recycle and push against global warming? What are our limits as humans? How can we work together to make rules against waste and financial risk, and to tax the richest countries to share wealth in solidarity with the poorest? We should also stop making disposable goods with planned obsolescence. We need to create useful things, without frivolity, to help the world's poorest. Yes, useful things to end world poverty. A thousand times more profitable than waging wars would be to implement practical rules for a fair economy for everyone on a planetary scale, to abolish the world's unfair economic competition and the miserable condition of poverty.

Perhaps our world needs fewer global organizations, forums and conferences, which just make hotel chains and airlines richer, and which often lack leadership to

foster real change. Yes, we need to think about what we have learned through history and from our ancestors so that, together with science, we can find solutions for humanity as a whole, instead of trying to make ourselves wealthier. Together with scientists, the first counselors of humanity, we should write agreements for the whole world. Rich nations and transnational corporations should not govern the human world, much less our financial system. That's right, I think we can find a solution in shared international politics, by working hand in hand with the scientific community to make political decisions for the world. But it should be a science that does not crave making a profit but

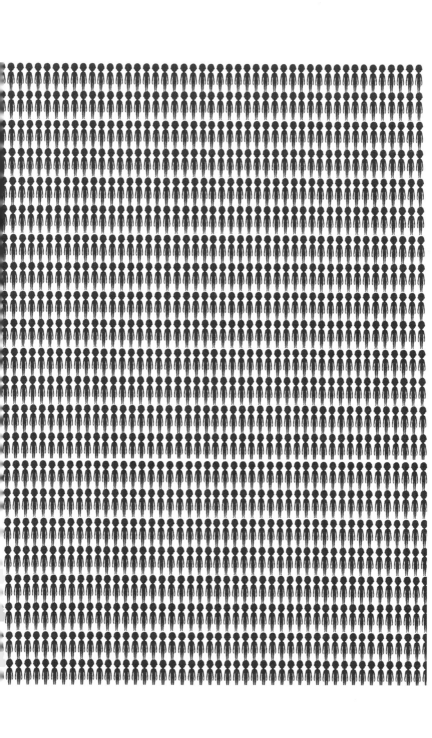

looks instead into the future and what could be, while warning us about those things that we are not paying attention to. How long ago was it that they warned us, during the Kyoto Climate Change Conference, about key problems we had not noticed? I believe that intelligence should drive us forward.

Such things, and others that I cannot elaborate on, seem essential, but they would require that we make life — not accumulation — the driving force.

Obviously, I am not that naive: these things will not happen immediately. We still need to make many sacrifices and repair what has been broken before being able to fix the root cause of our problems. Today the world is unable to regulate globalization on a planetary scale because international politics are weak. We will believe, for a while, in those regional agreements that make false promises about "free trade," but these will eventually end up building regional barriers all over the world. At the same time, we will see the growth of important industries and services, all dedicated to saving and renewing the environment. We will console ourselves thus for a while, we will keep ourselves entertained. And, of course, accumulation will continue unabated, to the delight of the financial system. Wars will continue, as well as fanaticism, until perhaps nature will call for order and make our civilization unviable. But let's avoid such negative, merciless views of seeing humans as the only species on Earth capable of going against its own species.

I will say it again, what some call the *planet's ecological crisis* is a consequence of the overwhelming triumph of human ambition. Ambition is our defeat, making us powerless to find answers in a new era that we have helped create. Why do I say this? Based on two simple facts: the truth is that the population has quadrupled, and the GDP has grown at least twentyfold in the last century. The world's trade has doubled approximately every six years since 1990. We could go on writing down data that clearly establishes the march of globalization. What is happening to us? We are entering this era at an accelerated pace, and we're doing so next to politicians, political parties, fake know-it-all celebrities and tired young people who must face a scary series of changes. These changes are happening so fast that it is impossible for us to understand them sometimes. We cannot

handle globalization because our thinking is not global. We're not sure if it's because of our cultural limitations or because we are reaching the limits of human biology.

Our era could be highly revolutionary, more than ever in the history of humankind. Yet we lack organized political leadership, conscious direction and the instinct to lead. We even lack a guiding philosophy to face the speed of accelerating change. Greed has been both a negative and a driving force of history. It has pushed us towards material, technical and scientific progress, making our era a phenomenal achievement on many fronts. It has also pushed us to domesticate

science and transform it into technology. Yet, paradoxically, greed is launching us into a historical abyss that we can't see and don't understand yet: an era without history. We are losing sight of things, and are left without collective intelligence to continue colonizing and perpetuating our transformation, because if there is one characteristic we share as little human bugs, it is that we are biologically driven to conquer.

We are increasingly being controlled by things that seem to have a life of their own. This gives us glimpses of the path ahead. But it has become impossible for us to collectivize global decisions for the sake of the *whole*. That is, individual greed has long triumphed over our higher greed of survival as a species. What do I mean when I say the whole? It has to do with planetary life on Earth, including human life, but with all the fragile balances in nature that make it possible for us to survive.

On the other hand — to say it in simpler, less opinionated

and clearer terms — particularly in the West, because that is where we come from, although we come from the South, republics were born to affirm that "all men are equal," that no one is greater than anyone else, and that governments should represent the common good, justice and equity. Many times, republics become distorted and invisible for everyday people. Republics were not created to run wild. On the contrary, they were historically created to make life functional for all, and, therefore, republics should be working to improve the lives of most people.

For whatever reason, because of our medieval beliefs in dividing people by class — which still exist — because of rich income groups that bully everyone or perhaps because of the consumerism around us: all republics often adopt a daily routine to distance themselves from regular people. When, in fact, they should be central to the republic's political struggle. Governments, republican governments, should increasingly resemble their people in the ways they live and the ways they commit themselves to care for life.

The fact is that we still hold old beliefs of kings and queens, of a wealthy class that "deserves

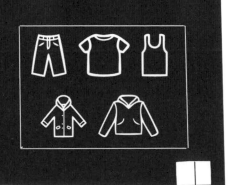

everything," thus creating hierarchies that undermine what republics were really created for: that we are all equal. The interplay of these and other factors keeps us in a prehistoric state, and today when all politics fail, we still resort to war. This is how the economy has been strangled. We waste our resources. Listen well, my dear friends: two million dollars are spent on the military per minute on this Earth, two million dollars per minute. It is spent on the military instead of on medical research for all illnesses, which has advanced enormously and is a blessing for increasing life expectancy, but comparatively, medical research barely covers one-fifth of what is

spent on military research. This endless process is blind, it leads to hatred and fanaticism, mistrust, generates more wars and wastes fortunes too.

I know that it is very easy to criticize humanity poetically, and I believe that it would be naive to suggest that there are enough resources in this world to be able to both save money and spend it on useful things. That would be possible, once again, if we could create world agreements and global planetary policies to secure peace, and to give the weakest countries guarantees they do not have. We would need to greatly cut back on wasteful resources and attend to the most urgent needs on Earth. We just need to ask ourselves: where would humanity be today without these planetary agreements? This is why everyone prepares for and agrees on the scale of war. And that is where we are today, because we cannot reason as a species, only as individuals.

Global institutions, particularly today, can't function under the shadow of great nations that say they disagree but obviously only care for holding on to their share of power. They block agreements in the United Nations, which was created as a beam of hope and a dream of peace for humankind. What is even worse, they uproot it from democracy, in a planetary sense. Because we are not equal, we cannot be equal in a world where there are stronger and weaker nations. Thus, we are left with a wounded and broken planetary democracy, without any real possibilities of a brave and resolute world peace agreement. We then try to heal wounds when they appear, but are overpowered by one or more of the stronger nations.

But what about the rest of us? We watch from afar, we do not exist. Friends, I believe it would be very difficult to invent a worse weapon than the aggressive nationalism that the strong nations use against others. Power can liberate the weak, and nationalism set us on the path of decolonization and can empower the weak. But both have been transformed into tools of oppression in the hands of the strong. The last two hundred years have given us plenty of examples everywhere!

THINK

The UN, our UN, is dying. It has been bureaucratized, lacks power, autonomy and recognition, and above all, is no longer a democratic space for the weak, which constitutes the planet's overwhelming majority. Let me give you a small, tiny example: of all Latin American countries, our small country has, in absolute terms, the largest presence of soldiers, scattered around the world, in peacekeeping missions. We go wherever they call us. But we are small, weak, and in those places where resources are distributed and decisions are made, we can't get through the door, not even to serve coffee.

Deep in our hearts there is a great desire to help humans emerge from prehistory. I believe that as long as we live in a state of war, we will continue to live in a prehistoric era, despite the many artifacts we might

build. The long journey and challenge ahead of us is for humankind to come out from that prehistory and stop using war as a resource when politics fails. And I say this knowing full well that war is desolation.

However, these dreams, these challenges we see on the horizon mean we need to fight for global agreements that can begin to govern our history and overcome, step by step, the imminent threats to life.

Our species should have one global government that fights for everyone on the planet and leaders who follow the path of science, instead of politicians and institutions that rule and suffocate us based on the needs of the few.

At the same time, we must understand that the world's poor are not just people from Africa or Latin America. The poor belong to a globalized humanity, and we must strive to help them so that families can live independently and with dignity. We have enough resources available, but they are being wasted by today's civilization. A few days ago in California, they paid tribute to an electric light bulb that has been burning in a fire station for one hundred years. A hundred years, my friends! How many millions of dollars have been drained from our pockets by deliberately making junk for people to buy, buy, and buy and buy and buy?

But our globalized desire of looking after the whole planet and all life in it means we need to make brutal cultural changes, which is what history needs from us. The material base on which society was built has changed and is teetering. Humankind remains frozen as if nothing has happened. And instead of governing globalization, globalization is governing us.

We have been arguing to instate the Tobin tax for over twenty years, but we have been unable to apply it on a global scale. All the banks and financial powers have resisted and made it impossible, claiming it would hurt them.

Nevertheless, through talent and collective work, and through science, humankind is capable of transforming deserts into green pastures. We can develop agriculture in the ocean. We can grow vegetables that live in salt water. Humankind's might, when focused on what is essential, is immeasurable. We could find the most magnificent sources of energy. What do we know about photosynthesis? Almost nothing. There is plenty of energy in the world if we worked with it and used it.

It is still possible to uproot all the poverty we see on the planet. It is possible to create stability, and future generations could bring life to the galaxy — if they managed to start reasoning as a species, not only as individuals — and pursue the dream of space exploration that all human beings carry in our genes.

But for all those dreams to become a reality, we need to govern ourselves. Or else we will succumb. Because we are not capable of living up to the civilization that we have been developing.

This is our dilemma. Let us avoid getting distracted by just repairing what has been broken. Let us think about the root causes, about how we consume and waste things, about our "use-and-throw-away" civilization, which is throwing away the time we have left as a species. Let's not waste this time on useless things. Just remember that human life is a miracle, that being alive is a miracle and that nothing is worth more than life. And that our biological duty, above all things, is to respect life and to drive it forward, take care of it, help it procreate and understand that the species is *all of us*.

Thank you.

KEYS TO THE SPEECH
A President Who Says What He Thinks

Commentary by Dolors Camats
Translated by Sofía Jarrin

On September 24, 2013, José "Pepe" Mujica spoke at the UN Member States annual meeting in New York. It was the 68th General Assembly of this international organization, which held its first session on January 10, 1946, in the same city, shortly after the end of World War II, with representatives from fifty-one countries.

During the first few days of the General Assembly, a designated amount of time is usually set aside for leaders of member states to deliver a speech. These speeches are free-themed to share something they consider significant about their country and of general interest to the other countries present.

In 2013, José Mujica, who was seventy-eight years old at the time and had been president of Uruguay for three years, spoke for forty-five minutes in his native language, Spanish, before a room prepared to welcome official representatives from 193 member states. The room was close to full.

José's speech began as expected for a head of state or a government representative at the UN. But the rest of his speech was unlike those usually heard at the United Nations Assembly, both in substance (what he said) and inflection (how he said it).

"I Am from the South, I Come from the South"

That day, some of those present said that while José was speaking, representatives of Latin American countries were smiling. They were pleased to see that his personal approach and critical opinions — on the effects of capitalism, globalization or nations' lack of interest in the problems of people around the world — did not change because he was in the presence of the people who governed those countries.

His Latin American colleagues — or, as he called them, compatriotas, from countries in the Americas that were colonized in the sixteenth century by Spain, Portugal or France, and where Spanish, Portuguese or French is now widely spoken — had already heard José speak at other events and knew that he is someone who says what he thinks, who prefers to share his thoughts, no matter how hard they may be to hear, rather than being looked at favorably or applauded. They were very familiar with his life, his political commitment to social justice and his struggle for equality and freedom. They knew the power of his words because they were spoken by someone whose words aligned with his actions.

"I am from the South, I come from the South." This is how he began his address.

He was referring thus not only to a geographical location — although Uruguay is indeed in South America — but to what it means to be and come from the South and the poor regions of the world, in the context of the United Nations.

Another Uruguayan, the poet Mario Benedetti, published a poem nearly forty years ago that became very popular called "El sur también existe" ("The South also exists"), which was later set to music by Joan Manuel Serrat. Benedetti also claimed the South as a territory of impoverished nations, which, instead of making their own decisions, had to adopt the decisions imposed on them by other governments which exploit their resources and wealth, and intervene to block or depose democratically elected governments.

The poem begins like this:

> with its rituals of steel
> its great chimneys
> its clandestine wise men
> its siren song
> its neon skies
> its christmas sales
> its worship of god the father
> and of epaulets
> with its keys to the kingdom
> the north is in command
>
> but down here
> hunger, readily at hand,
> resorts to taking the bitter fruit
> of what others decide
> while time passes by
> and parades go by
> and we do other things
> not sanctioned by the north
> with enduring hope
> the south also exists

"The World's Poorest President"

José takes pride in the fact that he is from the South. He also claims he belongs to the poor. In fact, during his term as Uruguay's president, his simple lifestyle, without any of the usual comforts or luxuries — so different from what people in government or with institutional power tend to have — led him to be known as "the world's poorest president."

When people would call him this, he would reply, "They say that I am a poor president. No, I am not a poor president. Poor are those who have more and yet, do not have enough. Those people are poor, because they get into an endless rat race and do not have time left for life nor anything else."

José lived modestly back then, as he still does, in a small house in a rural area of Montevideo, the country's capital, where he cultivates his vegetable garden with his wife Lucía Topolansky, the former vice-president of the Republic of Uruguay, and Manuela, their three-legged lap dog.

José became involved in political activism at a very young age. He later joined the National Liberation Movement, Tupamaros (MLN-T), named after Tupac Amaru, an Indigenous leader executed in Cuzco in 1781 for having rebelled against the Spanish colonizers.

The Tupamaros were a political movement, but also guerrillas that carried out violent actions such as kidnappings and armed robberies. When José says in his address, "The mistakes I made are partly a consequence of the times I had to live in," he is probably referring to his time as a guerrilla member, when he believed that violent actions were justified to defend his views of social justice and to oppose the government. José ended up being shot and wounded, imprisoned in jail but escaped soon after. He went underground and lived in hiding as a fugitive until he was arrested again.

José spent thirteen years in prison, from 1972 to 1985, not only as a prisoner but also as a hostage. The military government that had seized power in Uruguay arrested him and eight of his fellow Tupamaros, placed them in different facilities, and held them in solitary confinement, in inhumane, undignified conditions. On top of the psychological torture, there is evidence that they were physically abused during captivity (José was even locked up in a water tank). They were held under the threat that if the MLN-T acted violently again, they would be executed in response.

"Those years of solitude probably taught me the most. I went seven years without reading a book," José would share years later in an interview. "I had to rethink everything and learned to gallop inward at times, just so I wouldn't go crazy."

He and his companions were finally released in 1985 when democracy was restored, and José resumed his political activism as cofounder of a political party, the Movement of Popular Participation, which in turn gave rise to a unitary movement of left-wing parties, the Frente Amplio (Broad Front). The party defines itself as "progressive, democratic, popular, anti-oligarchic and anti-imperialist."

During this new period of political action, José held several positions as representative, senator, minister of agriculture and, finally, Uruguay's president for five years.

José is, therefore, a man who came from a radical armed struggle, survived torture and prison, to become a committed political militant within his party and the broader movement, and who has worked to govern and modernize his country and thus improve the lives of the poorest.

That day, in September 2013, José took the floor at the UN Assembly carrying this history on his back.

Who, What and How

During his address, José explained very eloquently the *who, what* and *how* of his thinking and the ideas that motivated him throughout his life, both in hiding and when he served as the country's president.

The Who. *Who does José speak for, who does he represent, and who does he want to defend.*

José was speaking on behalf of the most disadvantaged. When he was young, he believed that the most disadvantaged in his country were the peasants and workers, but he later realized that dispossessed Indigenous peoples and victims of all kinds of violence and exploitation in Latin America also suffered difficult living conditions that he wanted to change. That is why he tells us, "I see and feel responsible for the poverty of millions who live in urban areas, in the mountains, in the rainforests, in the pampas and in the underground mines of Latin America, a common homeland in the making."

During José's UN address, his *who* ends up being humankind or, as he likes to say, the entire human species. José defends the need to respect and care for all people, regardless of their origin or where they live. That is why, toward the end, he states that it is necessary to "understand that the species is *all of us.*"

The What. *Key ideas of how the world works, according to José.*

José takes advantage of having world leaders among his audience to make keen and direct criticisms against consumer capitalism. He makes it very clear when he says, "We have sacrificed old spiritual gods to adorn our temples with the God of the Market. He organizes our economy, politics, habits, life. He also gives us the illusion that happiness can be bought in installments and with credit cards."

By *capitalism*, we are talking about an economic and social system based on having private property and buying and selling goods and services with money as the source of wealth and exchange. When we speak of *consumer capitalism*, we refer to a system characterized by massive consumption of all kinds of resources, products and services, which constantly generates new needs.

The How. *José's recommendations for the kind of tools we need to change the world.*

José's speech is a call to raise awareness. He wants us to realize that our lifestyle (how we make a living, what we spend our money on, the needs or desires we create) and our collective organization (where we get our resources from, how we spend them, how wealth is distributed in each country) have effects on the lives of others and on the planet.

José asks the representatives of those nations, and all of us, to make a commitment. He says we should not be merely driven by our own self-interests, that we should not remain passive when confronted with the problems and injustices that affect us all. He lives by example through his political commitment: a simple life, the need for very few things and a political stance that strives to be close to and useful to the people, changing the root causes of problems, worrying about the common good and the needs of the planet, and making it clear that he will not, under any circumstances, be bought by the market economy nor by the power of money.

Consumerism Makes Us Less Free

José defends his simple way of living and the way it is closely linked to his desire to be a free man, saying, "It would seem we were born to consume and consume and, when we can no longer consume, we are overcome with frustration, poverty and even self-isolation." In another interview he states, "If I own a few things, I need little to sustain them. ... Therefore, the time I dedicate to them is minimal. And what do I then have time left for? To spend it on the things I like. At that moment, I believe I am free."

José condemns this paradox: in today's world we can produce more and better, we have greater scientific technology and we have more resources than at any other time in history. Yet all these improvements and advances, instead of making us happier and helping us work toward solving humanity's most pressing problems, just generate greater needs that lead to greater frustration. This increases inequalities between people and regions of the world and leads to wasted resources, pollution and climate change.

One way to understand José's meaning is to look at the story he shares about the light bulb in the firehouse in Livermore, California, which has been burning since 1901. Made of a semiconductor material and an extra-thick filament, this bulb has been burning for more than a million hours without going out. The latest LED bulbs on the market are designed to last approximately fifty thousand hours, while the old incandescent bulbs we still have in our homes do not last more than a thousand hours.

Does this mean that a hundred years ago they made better light bulbs than today? No. It means that today's bulbs, like so many other things, are designed to stop working after a certain period of time (decided by the manufacturer). This is called *planned obsolescence*. The objective is very easy to understand if we think about the manufacturer's interests, or the company that sells the product. It seeks to generate a need in the customer, who is forced to replace the product with a new one, buy it again, which will then increase the company's income. The purpose of obsolescence is not to create better-quality products or to guarantee satisfying our real needs, but to secure economic gain. Not to mention that they do not care about wasting resources, generating waste and pollution. Much of our current economic system is based on this, and José denounces it bluntly, because it goes against all logic and against the preservation of natural resources and, above all, because it condemns people to unnecessary consumption that ends up making them unhappy: "How many millions of dollars have been drained from our pockets by deliberately making junk for people to buy, buy, and buy and buy and buy?"

José also takes the opportunity to denounce what he considers to be the greatest waste of all, the most useless of all useless expenditures: military spending on armament. As long as war is a resource, he says, humanity will live in prehistory. We must think on benefitting the world's population instead of the interests of one or a few countries. José criticizes the stance of great economic powers, countries that control the international system. They have power over what happens beyond their borders, but if they are not interested in a particular issue, they can make it or the country invisible.

Against the Globalized Economy, Against Global Government

"But today is the time to start fighting back, to make way for a world without borders ... More clearly, let's say it more clearly: we believe that the world is crying out for global rules that respect scientific achievements, but science does not govern the world." José speaks about the need to bring order to globalization. By *globalization* we mean the process whereby regional economies, societies and cultures around the world are integrated into a worldwide network of communications, transportation and trade. Globalization doesn't allow for a single clear leadership. Instead, large multinational corporations and international banks make decisions that benefit only themselves, while directly affecting people's lives and the planet's resources. National governments can no longer prevent this, and they sometimes even help to implement these decisions.

We can experience this in our daily lives. If we walk around any big city in the world, it is likely that wherever we go we will find the same stores we are already familiar with. We may even hear the same music inside them. But do you think the working conditions for those employees are the same everywhere? Do they have to work just as long for the same pay, or do their wages and working hours change from country to country around the world? If we allow trade to have free rein, should we not allow workers' rights to be internationalized as well?

In his speech, José calls for a government that makes these decisions at the international level, that regulates how citizens are impacted around the world, and that takes into account their real needs and not those of big business. Such a government should be governed by politics, based on science and logic, and be at the service of the common good.

Others have already spoken out against the misgovernment or ill-governance of globalization before. In 2001, in the Brazilian city of Porto Alegre, more than 12,000 people from all over the world gathered during the first meeting of the World Social Forum, concerned about the effects of globalization on people's lives, minority cultures and the environment. In the years that followed, an alternative movement to corporate globalization, known as the anti-globalization or alter-globalization movement, was organized under the slogan "Another world is possible."

The World Social Forum is a space for generating and debating alternative proposals. One of the first and main proposals was the demand for the implementation of the Tobin tax.

The idea behind the Tobin tax is to levy a tax on each financial transaction (money or foreign currency exchange), which would be collected internationally (instead of by a single country). Imagine, for example, a European bank that buys millions of US dollars because this currency is cheap at the moment, sells them a few days (or a few hours!) later and makes lots of money. The Tobin tax would be applied on currency transactions like this, and some of the money collected could be used to benefit developing countries or to fight climate change.

As José reminds us, "We have been arguing to instate the Tobin tax for over twenty years, but we have been unable to apply it on a global scale. All the banks and financial powers have resisted and made it impossible, claiming it would hurt them."

The proposed duty has yet to be applied, although it has been discussed not only by the anti-globalization movement but also by some nations, especially in the European Union and Latin America.

This and other proposals are on the table. José demands that we put these bold policies into practice.

Against Ambition and Waste: Austerity and Ecology

"The truth is that today, if everyone consumed like the average person in the United States, we would need three planets to survive. In other words, we have been tricked by the promises of our civilization." What are the limits of our planet if we all consume like those living in the richest countries? What are the limits of water, of the natural resources needed to produce everything we need, of the food we consume, and of the impact of our activities on the air we breathe? What are the effects on the rest of humanity that cannot access our level of consumption, the impact on other living beings on the planet, or the impact on the climate?

José proposes that we change, that we stop this senseless and ever-growing consumption, which does not lead us to happiness. And he asks us to act to preserve and take care of the planet because it is the only planet we have. José proposes that we live more simply, with austerity.

As a result of the 2008 financial crisis that affected the richest countries' economies and, in turn, a large part of the financial system — that is, the banks and the global economic system — many governments, especially those from the European Union, implemented so-called *austerity* measures. A little over fifteen years ago, they came out in defense of this concept as a synonym for reducing (or cutting) government spending, which also affected investments in services that help reduce social inequalities, that is, everything that contributes to cover people's basic needs (housing, health, education, etc.) regardless of how much money they have.

But this is not the austerity José is advocating for. He is referring to the kind of austerity another politician called for, many years earlier. In 1977, Enrico Berlinguer, secretary-general of the Italian Communist Party, gave a speech addressed to his party members. Back then, Europe was also experiencing an economic crisis, and Berlinguer defended austerity as an ideal central element in the operating model of our societies. He thought it could lead people away from the economic model that dominated back then — a model that wasted energy and material resources, spurred out-of-control consumption and an individualism that worked against the common good. Does this remind you of what José said thirty-six years later?

Maybe the tone of his speech — somewhere between a complaint and "enough is enough!" — has a lot to do with the fact that his criticism of what was no longer working was nothing new: "How long ago was it that they warned us during the Kyoto Climate Change Conference about key problems we had not noticed?"

The Kyoto Protocol was an international agreement that aimed to reduce emissions of six greenhouse gases that contribute to climate change. It was launched in 1997 in Kyoto, Japan, and almost all the countries in the world signed on to it. Since 2020, the Kyoto Protocol has been replaced by the Paris Agreement as the main international climate agreement. However, the main emitters of greenhouse gases have few intentions of committing to the signed agreement.

Scientific evidence shows that over the last fifty years human activities have contributed to climate change. These activities include mostly coal, oil, and gas combustion, as well as deforestation and intensive agriculture.

In view of this, José urges us not to be guided by accumulation or consumption when making decisions, but to think of *all of us*, to preserve and care for life.

What Do You Think?

José's UN address is easy to understand. He speaks passionately and uses facts from his life and his own experiences to make it engaging. Sometimes he even adopts a poetic tone. And he refers to issues that are not normally discussed at the United Nations: love, life, free time, the defense of authority and criticisms of squandering and excessive consumerism.

On the other hand, his words are also harsh and direct, and sometimes they even convey anger. He uses powerful expressions to make an impact, and he likes to challenge people using the authority of his many years of experience. He himself says that perhaps he is too defeatist. But is he pessimistic? José is a man in his eighties who assumes responsibility for his past, not an easy past, who criticizes our present day for the injustice and lack of solidarity it represents, and, at the same time, is concerned about the future of humanity. Maybe he is indeed pessimistic, but he is also a fighter, someone who practices what he preaches, and he has always thought that making an effort to improve people's lives is worthwhile.

Source Notes

Page 46: Benedetti, Mario. "El sur también existe." Preguntas al azar. Visor Libros: Spain, 2001.

Page 47: "Las frases más memorables de Mujica." *YouTube*, uploaded by BBC News Mundo, 1 March 2015.

Page 48: "La entrevista de José - URUGUAY - #HUMAN." *YouTube*, uploaded by HUMAN la pelicula, 2 August 2016.

Page 48: "Estatutos." Frente Amplio. *Frente Amplio*, 12 Dec. 2019. Online.

Page 52: "Salvados - José Mujica habla sobre el consumismo." *YouTube*, uploaded by laSexta, 19 May 2014.

Also in the Speak Out series

Severn Speaks Out

**Speech by Severn Cullis-Suzuki • Analysis by Alex Nogués
Translated by Susan Ouriou • Illustrations by Ana Suárez**

Before Greta Thunberg there was Severn Cullis-Suzuki, whose 1992 Earth Summit speech made her known as "the girl who silenced the world for five minutes."

Hardcover jacket: 978-1-77306-887-9   Ebook: 978-1-77306-888-6

The first section of the work can be used in speech classes, and both portions offer eye-opening lessons in social justice and environmentalism. . worthwhile purchase for classrooms and libraries." — *Booklist*

Malala Speaks Out

Speech by Malala Yousafzai • Commentary by Clara Fons Duocastella • Translated by Susan Ouriou • Illustrations by Yael Frankel

Malala Yousafzai was denied education when the Taliban took control of her town in Pakistan. She decided to speak up, despite the danger it put her in. Her story is the story of many girls.

Hardcover jacket: 978-1-77306-916-6   Ebook: 978-1-77306-917-3

By almost any measure, Malala's speech is inspiring. … This speech is worthy of highlighting to a larger audience, and *Malala Speaks Out* will make great addition to social justice units." — *CM: Canadian Review of Materials*

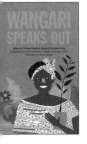

Wangari Speaks Out

Speech by Wangari Maathai • Commentary by Laia de Ahumada • Translated by Susan Ouriou • Illustrations by Vanina Starkoff

Wangari Maathai started the Green Belt Movement, which has planted tens of millions of trees. She was the first African woman and first environmentalist to receive a Nobel Peace Prize.

Hardcover jacket: 978-1-77306-956-2   Ebook: 978-1-77306-957-9

Groundwood Books is grateful for the opportunity
to share stories and make books on the Traditional
Territory of many Nations, including the Anishinabeg,
the Wendat and the Haudenosaunee. It is also the
Treaty Lands of the Mississaugas of the Credit. In
partnership with Indigenous writers, illustrators, editors
and translators, we commit to publishing stories that
reflect the experiences of Indigenous Peoples.
For more about our work and values, visit us at
groundwoodbooks.com.